Original title:
Where Walls Have Stories

Copyright © 2025 Creative Arts Management OÜ
All rights reserved.

Author: Adrian Caldwell
ISBN HARDBACK: 978-1-80587-115-6
ISBN PAPERBACK: 978-1-80587-585-7

The Diary of Dust and Light

In shadows thick with tales untold,
Laughed a dust bunny, brave and bold.
It claimed a throne, a faded shoe,
And whispered secrets, just for a few.

The sunbeams danced, a merry crew,
While cobwebs swayed like curtains too.
A mouse took notes, all ears and eyes,
As dust shared dreams of pizza pies.

Each crack and crevice held a scream,
Of an old sock that once walked the seam.
The paint peeled back, its stories grow,
Of kids who painted the walls with woe.

With giggles echoing through the night,
The walls confided in moon's soft light.
Though lessons learned may fade with time,
These whispers linger, pure comic rhyme.

Tales Carved in Stone

In a house built on laughs, bricks have a quirk,
They whisper of ghosts who loved to smirk.
The windows roll eyes, panes play a joke,
Every door creaks out loud when folks poke.

In the hallway, shadows dance with flair,
While a picture frame grins with a flair.
A cat that once lived, now just an outline,
Claims the best spots and calls it divine.

The Language of Echoed Footsteps

Every step is a giggle, knocks on the floor,
Telling the tales of the fun days before.
Squeaky sneakers and boots stampede,
Communicating secrets that neighbors don't heed.

In the echo, a rumor, a faint little call,
'Did you hear about the cake? She slipped, took a fall!'
Creaky old steps joined in with a shout,
And the walls chuckle softly, knowing all about.

Memories Etched in Wood

On polished old panels, stories conspire,
Each scratch and each dent held laughter, not fire.
A squirrel's bold heist, a cat's floppy leap,
The furniture giggles, they've secrets to keep.

Cozy chairs cringe from the weight of the tales,
Of kids tied with ribbons setting off on their sails.
Riddles wrapped tightly in fibers and knots,
Waiting for visitors to share all their thoughts.

Silence Spun in Threads of Wallpaper

Draped in a pattern both wondrous and bold,
Old wallpaper chuckles at secrets retold.
The flowers are gossiping, petals aflame,
As the wallpaper blushes with stories of shame.

In corners, the creases wear laughter like hats,
While dust bunnies dance with the occasional cat.
Stuck under the surface, this fun never ends,
For behind every layer, a new tale extends!

Unraveled Threads of Heritage

In the attic, lost socks await,
Their missing mates, a tangled fate.
Grandma laughs, and the cat takes a nap,
While history's spun from yarn and flap.

Old photos peek from a dusty shoe,
Gramps with a hairdo, oh my, who knew?
Pants that once fit are now quite absurd,
As stories of laughter escape, unheard.

The Song of Faded Colors

Paint drips down like old gossip flow,
On walls that once glowed in vibrant show.
A mural of kids playing leapfrog,
Now they just lounge, like a tired old dog.

The colors all faded, a quiet retreat,
Yet laughter still echoes with rhythm, a beat.
As grandma hums tunes of a paint-splattered life,
The walls shimmy joyfully, causing no strife.

Tales Written in Dust

Dust settles thick on that chair in the hall,
Holding the secrets of those who would sprawl.
A wise old mouse knows more than you think,
About the late-night snacks shared over a drink.

Cobwebs weave stories of long-lost fads,
Records of parties, of the shy and the jads.
The vacuum's a villain, but it won't erase,
The laughter and chaos, the cluttered embrace.

Narratives in the Grain

Each creak in the floorboards tells tales at night,
Of long-lost lovers who danced in the light.
The furniture squeaks with old jokes to share,
As dust bunnies giggle without a care.

Worn-out chairs hold the weight of their dreams,
While shadows of children create joyful schemes.
In the grain of the wood, memories merge,
As laughter and whimsy begin to surge.

The Ghosts of Laughter and Tears

In corners, giggles haunt the halls,
While shadows dance as evening falls.
A cat with attitude, so sly,
Claims the couch as its throne nearby.

Old photos wink with smirks and grins,
Reminding us of all our sins.
The squeak of floors, a playful tease,
As memories swirl like autumn leaves.

Footprints of Those Who Were

The floors groan under secret chats,
As mice scurry, plotting their spats.
Each footprint tells a tale or two,
Of clumsy dances and silly whoops, too.

Invisible pranks stretch across the night,
With laughter echoing, oh what a sight!
Each room a canvas, vibrant and bright,
Painted with moments—what pure delight!

Residue of Rainy Days

Raindrops trickle, a pitter patter,
As children laugh with socks in tatters.
Puzzle pieces scattered 'round,
In that chaos, joy is found.

Umbrellas flipped, much to our glee,
As puddles become our own marquee.
Footprints squish with every leap,
In this rainy world, fun's our keep.

Secrets Slow to Fade

Beneath the plaster, whispers snooze,
Of pranks played and silly ruse.
Each crack reveals a smirk or wink,
In old kitchens where we'd never think.

Forgotten toys, in dust they slay,
Chasing sunlight through shades of gray.
Secrets linger like a ghostly jest,
In these walls, we feel so blessed.

Legends Written in Dust

In corners thick with ancient dust,
The tales spin round, oh how they must!
A cat that stole the baker's pie,
With witnesses, they giggle and sigh.

Each layer thick holds tales untold,
Of brave young knights and treasures bold.
But who really believes the tales we weave?
A dust bunny knight? You've gotta believe!

The Weight of Buried Histories

Beneath the floor, a treasure lies,
Or maybe just old lunch with flies.
A sandwich sealed in time's embrace,
Legend says it won a race!

With every creak a secret's shared,
Of lovers caught who never dared.
The walls don't care, they just stand tall,
While ghosts of awkward dates have a ball.

Windowpanes Capturing Lost Moments

A smear of jam, a child's handprint,
The stories pressed, no hint to stint.
A nose pressed flat, faces all aglow,
While neighborhood gossip starts to flow.

Through panes so smudged, a view divine,
Birds pose for selfies, not a dull line.
They caw of love, of food, of fun,
These moments caught, oh what a run!

Dreams Embedded in Brick

In bricks that dream, plans start to hatch,
Of pizza parties, and a wildmatch.
Caught in the strength of mortar's grasp,
A giant mouse? "Don't eat my rasp!"

With each brick laid, new hopes arise,
Of chocolate rivers and endless fries.
The day is bright, yet walls hold tight,
To dreams of fun that take to flight!

Textures of Time Unraveled

In a house of creaky floors,
Ghosts juggle socks and chores.
A cat named Whiskers tells a tale,
Of mice that giggled and hurried pale.

Old paintings wink with a sly grin,
As dust bunnies race to sneak in.
Chairs dance while no one's around,
Whispers of laughter in every sound.

Tales Hidden Between the Lines

Books stacked high, what a sight,
Spiders plot in the dead of night.
The pages hum with secrets kept,
While the ink gets up and has a pep!

A dictionary sings sonnets anew,
As thieves steal words just for a view.
Puns linger like fragrant bread,
With giggles and snickers in the head.

The Resonance of Old Steps

In the hall, shoes shuffle in rhyme,
Tapping out beats, frozen in time.
Each squeak and creak holds a dance,
As the stairs laugh, giving a chance.

A sock puppet saunters back,
Making a case for each little crack.
With jokes carved in the bannister's wood,
The staircase grins, it's understood.

Memories in the Mortar

Brick walls whisper in the night,
Tickling tales of a goofy kite.
They've seen socks tossed in the air,
And ice cream spills without a care.

Each stone a friend with a million laughs,
Reciting mishaps and random gaffes.
The laughter echoes, never to fade,
In memories layered and humor displayed.

Chronicles Beneath the Ceiling

In the attic, dust bunnies play,
Claiming the beams, they joke all day.
A squirrel's wardrobe made of rags,
Dances with shadows in playful gags.

The spider spins tales from tangled threads,
While whispers of secrets rest in their beds.
The creaky floorboards laugh and squeak,
As ghosts of the past join in to peek.

Tapestries of Time

Stitched into fabric, tales arise,
Of a cat who wore sunglasses and flies.
Knitted by grandmas on chilly nights,
Each loop holds a giggle; oh what sights!

A rogue sock thief, it's said, took flight,
With a pair of shoes, oh what a sight!
They roam the halls in a comical chase,
Creating a scene, a slapstick grace.

The Stories in the Shadows

In corners dark, the dust bunnies meet,
To spin their yarns about lost socks' defeat.
A shimmery mouse with a twinkle in eye,
Tells tales of the cheese that managed to fly!

The shadows chuckle, the moonlight beams,
They share wild wishes, outrageous dreams.
All tucked away in a cozy nook,
Life's merry mischief is off the hook.

Legends of Old Beams

The beams overhead, they whisper and tease,
Remembering times of liver sausages with cheese.
A raccoon in a hat and a pair of shoes,
Claims to be royalty, and sings the blues!

Old chairs creak in laughter, a pleasant sort,
Echoing legends, a jubilant sport.
With every crevice, a cackle or two,
The tales of mischief in every view.

The Heartbeat of Old Structures

Creaking floors are laughing here,
Whispers come and disappear,
Nosey nails poke tales in wood,
Riddles shared where silence stood.

Chairs that squeak in echo's tune,
Tell me stories, afternoons,
Plumbing groans in playful jest,
Every crack, a secret quest.

Windows wink, with paint so bright,
Old jokes linger in the light,
Foxes scamper through the halls,
Chasing memories in old walls.

Each room grins with tales untold,
Of mismatched socks and spoons of gold,
The walls chuckle, not a fright,
History's fun, a true delight.

Timeworn Echoes

Echoes bounce on dusty beams,
While secrets dance in daylight dreams,
Hiccups of the past persist,
With giggles hidden in the mist.

Cracks in plaster spin a yarn,
Lighting bolts along the barn,
The kitchen hums a quirky tune,
Where spoons tap half a tune in June.

Old books laugh with stories old,
Their pages crinkle, tales retold,
The shadows tell of pranks once played,
And every corner's now displayed.

Dust bunnies bounce with glee and fright,
In the glow of soft moonlight,
Even cobwebs, with a jig,
Join the dance, oh, what a gig!

Secrets Beneath the Paint

Layers thick with laughs and sighs,
Every brush stroke hides a surprise,
Underneath this fickle coat,
Lies a frog or a castle moat.

Faces trapped in faded hue,
Mothers scolded, lovers too,
Fingers smeared on every wall,
Stories baked in summer's crawl.

Colorful schemes in playful jest,
Swirls that put time to the test,
Patchy spots hold laughter tight,
Whispers glide in the twilight.

Sneaky spots where mischief grew,
Paint spills tell of moments true,
As you wipe away the grime,
You may find a giggle's rhyme.

The Ghosts of Room Corners

In every corner, shadows play,
Whispers of a bygone day,
With a wink, they make you laugh,
As they take their ghostly bath.

Chandeliers hum a jolly tune,
While specters dance beneath the moon,
Puppets strut with silent glee,
In rooms where spirits roam so free.

Through cobwebs, secrets softly twine,
Phantoms sip on aged moonshine,
Even the dust has got a thought,
Laughter echoes, time forgot.

Though they glide with spooky grace,
In their hearts, they know their place,
To fill the night with mirthful cheer,
Ghosts are funny, it's crystal clear!

Echoes in the Plaster

In the corner, a shoe has settled,
A dance partner, quite unmeddled.
The frame creaks with glee, no doubt,
As the mouse twirls about, no one shouts.

Chili on Taco Tuesday flung,
Paint says, "Some stories aren't sung!"
Nail holes giggle at past mishaps,
Each ghostly laugh wraps like old wraps.

Beneath the drapes, a tale unfolds,
Of gnomes who stole the neighbor's gold!
And the cat, oh how it did plot,
To track down snacks in that very spot.

Oh, the walls tell tales, oh so bold,
Of a sock thief whose heart turned cold.
Or a cactus that won a sign debate,
In the realm of old chair fate.

Secrets Beneath the Paint

Under layers of robin egg blue,
Lies a story that could make you rue.
An artist's brush went a bit awry,
Made the cat look like a pie!

Each drip and drop a tale of woe,
Why did the curtains seem to glow?
With laughter echoing through the crack,
It whispers, "Let's never look back!"

A turtle raced a snail last spring,
And the door saw them both bling.
The floorboards squeaked with a snort,
As a roach carried a popcorn sort.

Oh, the paint is where secrets hide,
In a world of mischief, they abide.
The wallpaper's wild, a dance so surreal,
Every flake a chuckle, oh what a reel!

Whispers of Time Within

In the attic, a clock has stopped,
But the story's still hot and dropped.
With each tick, a rumor spins,
Like how Uncle Bob lost his wins.

The wallpaper peels with a grin,
Saying, "Let the fun begin!"
A painting of an old dear cat,
Who plotted attacks with just a bat.

From the cellar below, laughter rings,
Of hidden socks and their springs.
The dust bunnies dance in a line,
Making mischief as they entwine.

The tales circle like a playful breeze,
Of knock-knock jokes and tiny fleas.
In corners and nooks, they all conspire,
To keep the mood light, never tire!

Shadows of Abandoned Dreams

In a corner, where shadows play,
Lies a bicycle, dreamed away.
With a wobbly wheel, it would go,
But only on days with no snow!

A doll once twinkled in the sun,
Now haunting games of pretend fun.
It whispers of tea parties galore,
Despite the ants trying to score.

The curtains sway with a sneaky nod,
To secrets shared with the odd.
You'll find capers, quite absurd,
Of a bat who fancied a card bird.

Abandoned dreams hold whims galore,
They sparkle and giggle, wanting more.
For in silence, laughter breaks free,
Echoing softly, a grand decree!

The Heart of the Abandoned

In a house that once had charm,
Rats hold meetings without alarm.
The creaky floorboards tell a tale,
Of a lost cat who went on bail.

Paint peels in colors bright and bold,
Once vibrant tales, now quiet and old.
A ghost of a dog with a wagging tail,
Still guards the snacks that never fail.

Empty bottles line the shelves,
Each a story, like sage elves.
A chair sits dusty in the light,
Still waiting for someone to ignite.

In every dent and peeling wall,
The laughter of echoes still does call.
Though overgrown, it wears a crown,
This place of dreams won't wear a frown.

Liquid Layers of Memory

In cups of dust, memories steep,
Forgotten secrets, none to keep.
Tea stains swirl in patterns grand,
Of invisible friends, hand in hand.

The sink holds whispers, soft and slick,
Of kitchen mishaps, a shift and a flick.
Spilled soup and laughter, right on cue,
A culinary drama, oh so true!

Bubbles rise from the unknown,
Counting the days this house has grown.
Old recipes in jars abound,
A comedic masterpiece, all around.

In every splash and every swirl,
There's a joke the old tap would unfurl.
Liquid laughter, echoes in streams,
As we relish our whimsical dreams.

Ghostly Intrigues of Dwelling Spaces

In the corners, shadows lurk,
Specters giggle, it's a quirky perk.
They plot their pranks with glee and cheer,
Turning stale bread into a souvenir!

The windows chatter with tales of fright,
Of poor souls jumping at every slight.
Curtains swirl as if to tease,
While the ghosts dance away with ease.

In every crack, a secret hides,
A door that creaks, where laughter abides.
Echoes of dramas, mishaps galore,
From the fun times when they lived before.

With each batty thump and rattle,
The night becomes a playful battle.
These hauntings are not grim or dire,
They spark the fun, we can't retire!

Pockets of Time

In closets deep, old coats are lost,
Each pocket contains tales of cost.
A missing sock, a rumbling phone,
Chronicles of lives that have overgrown.

Beneath the stairs, a dust-filled chest,
Holds knick-knacks from a family quest.
A rubber duck that once could float,
Now a relic, wearing a joke's coat.

Hidden beneath a mattress firm,
Are notes of love, twisted and wormed.
Each scribble sings of silly dreams,
In the squishy mosh of childhood schemes.

Time slips through the creaks and cracks,
With giggles wrapped in playful hacks.
These pockets share what we cannot dare,
A funny glimpse of time left bare.

Stories Suspended in Cobwebs

In the corner, dust bunnies leap,
Caution tape wrapped tight, silence to keep.
Laughter trapped in spider's snack,
All those jokes that never came back.

Ghosts of giggles hover near,
Dotting the air with friendly cheer.
Tickling memories tangled around,
As we dance through laughter unbound.

Cracks in the plaster share a grin,
Echoing laughter beneath the skin.
If walls could laugh, they surely would,
Giggling at all that we thought was good.

Dusty diaries in shadows hide,
Whispering tales with a playful stride.
Give me a flower, I'll give you a jest,
In this comedy club, we're all just guests.

The Symphony of Unspoken Words

In the hallway, echoes burst forth,
Whispers of gossip, a real worth.
Each creak of the floor tells a tale,
Of awkward moments where friendships pale.

Chairs squeak a tune, in fractured rhyme,
Bouncing thoughts, lost in the grime.
Curtains shimmer with secrets dense,
Stories written with laughter and suspense.

A nod from the chair, a wink from the wall,
Signaling gossip, they've heard it all.
A symphony plays, in giggles and sighs,
Unspoken words fly into the skies.

With every whisper, a note ascends,
A harmony built on laughter, friends.
In the silence, let's all raise a toast,
To unshared laughs, we cherish the most.

Echoes in the Gaps

In the gaps of the roof, a secret resides,
Whispering jokes where the air collides.
Laughter trapped in the hollows of space,
As we search for smiles, in every place.

Underneath tiles, a chuckle resides,
Waiting for moments when humor collides.
Each crack in the walls sings, 'Let's have fun,'
Mimicking laughter until the day's done.

A fleeting whisper, a silly pun,
Echoes of laughter from everyone.
When you check the corners, feel the cheer,
You'll stumble on tales always near.

In shadows and crevices, friends unite,
Bantering softly, tucked out of sight.
Every corner, a giggly chat,
Dodging the serious, just like that!

Whispers of the Past

Under the stairs, giggles abide,
Late-night secrets, nowhere to hide.
In the wallpaper, stories overlap,
Funny moments in a cozy lap.

Tickling echoes of mischief prevail,
Old sock puppets dust off their tale.
Each word a bubble, waiting to pop,
Floating on memories, they never stop.

Whispers that tickle, a charm so sweet,
In narrow halls, friendships repeat.
The portraits wink, as we stroll by,
Telling the tales they wish to defy.

Old chairs are brimming with laughter stored,
While dusty old books simply hoard.
In this playful retreat, we all partake,
Our joy's the story that never will break.

Epilogues in the Corners

In the corner, a shoe with no pair,
Whispers of where it went, unaware.
A chair with a tale of a cat in a hat,
Spinning yarns of a time gone flat.

Next to it sits an old rubber duck,
Counting the days, like it's out of luck.
It quacks at the walls, a great comedy show,
Turning history's frown into a big glowing 'Whoa!'

A broom in the closet, dreaming of flight,
Imagining dust motes as stars of the night.
It sweeps up the stories from floor to the sky,
Occasional sneezes, "I think I might die!"

Old wallpaper peels, revealing a grin,
Chasing memories that once crept in.
It's a comedy club for garments and grime,
Each layer a joke, punchlines lost in time.

Secrets Cradled in Dust Motifs

Dust bunnies roll like they own the day,
Hiding their treasures in a playful display.
A sock that once danced, now under the bed,
Imagining parties, missed socks left for dead.

A forgotten toy soldier, dust on its shield,
Dreaming of battles it never revealed.
Giggling with echoes from ages gone past,
It's planning a comeback, a blast from the blast.

Sticky notes peeking like spies on the wall,
Recalling the pranks in the great dusty hall.
"Remember when you dared me to eat that pie?"
Invisible laughter, makes walls sigh and cry.

A chandelier sways, reminiscent of glee,
Swaying to tales of old jubilee.
It softens the light to let rumors drift,
The grandest of secrets, still waiting for gifts.

The Multitude of Human Footprints

Footprints traipse through hallways like gigs in a park,
Each step a memory, leaving its mark.
One leads to the fridge for a midnight snack,
While another veers off—oh, what a track!

A mini-sandwich, stuck under the rug,
Claims to be gourmet—a fine dining smug.
Yet ants have a party, all dressed up for fun,
Toast crumbs await in this lively run.

A giant's bootprint left in the dust,
Dwarfs all the others, but who can we trust?
It tells quite a yarn, with each slip and slide,
A tale of adventure that can't be denied.

Squirrels' soft paw prints sneak through the door,
Chasing the echoes from days of yore.
They scamper and scurry, never feeling sore,
In a game of hide-and-seek, a real folklore.

Imprints of Peace and Turmoil

On the walls are scuffles and laughter alike,
Witnessing squabbles and the odd little bike.
A dent from a tantrum, a thumbprint of cheer,
Each shows a moment, some far and some near.

Graffiti of memories, scribbled with pride,
The wall's a collector, with stories to hide.
A heart drawn with marker, once bold, now a frown,
Tells of young love, that leap and that drown.

Tea stains next to tears, a marbling dance,
Unraveled love stories, no second chance.
Yet the sun shines brightly on every mistake,
Turning each moment to laughter's sweet break.

Echoes of footsteps, in harmony swell,
Whispers of peace in the chaos they tell.
The walls might get weary, and yet they stay true,
Holding laughter close, like a warm morning dew.

Resonance of Lives Intertwined

In the corner, a cat naps tight,
Next to a shoe with a terrible bite.
Old photos dance on the crumbling wall,
As dust bunnies plot their next great fall.

A squeaky floor tells tales of glee,
Of kids and their snacks, as happy as can be.
A haphazard pirate map on the fridge,
Leads to the secrets of the old wooden bridge.

Loud parties echoed until the dawn,
Traces of laughter linger and yawn.
The clock with a quirk ticks in delight,
Whispers of chaos on cold, starry nights.

Amidst the chatter, and pots that clank,
A figment of whimsy in a heart-shaped tank.
These walls might hold stories, quirky and bright,
Of life's little mischiefs, a delightful sight.

Footprints of Forgotten Dreams

Under the bed lies an old, dusty shoe,
Once a soft slipper, now a hard hullabaloo.
Dreams of sailing on the high seas ablaze,
Now just a dust cloud in a hazy maze.

Forgotten sock puppets with lost conversation,
Rehearsing their lines for a grand separation.
Chairs that squeak as they gossip away,
Telling tall tales of yesterday's play.

An umbrella with a hole claims it's a sail,
While rubber duckies plot their next big tale.
The walls chuckle softly, a secretive crew,
As echoes of laughter dance with a view.

Under the layers of grime and cheer,
Lie whimsical footnotes of all that appears.
In a world of hiccups and giggles so wide,
These footprints tell stories we can't seem to hide.

Strains of Lost Laughter

A creaky door with its whimsical squeak,
Hums the melody of a jester's cheek.
In the breeze, a whoopee cushion still sings,
Of laughter that bursts like the silliest things.

The old rocking chair rocks back in time,
To the rhythm of jokes and slip-ups sublime.
In the kitchen, a pot makes a bubble and pop,
As noodles giggle in a cartoonish hop.

Jokes etched in wood, some silly, some sly,
While a clever owl hoots from the nearby sky.
Each window a canvas, each frame a delight,
Recalling the antics each fun-loving night.

From puns to pratfalls, a whimsical trove,
Of laughter that spills like a rich, hearty grove.
What stories unfold in the sunshine's glow,
As the echoes of chuckles put on a show.

Fortunes in Faded Tiles

The tiles below sport a patchwork of hues,
Cracked riddles of life and mismatched shoes.
Stories of spills and chips that reveal,
The feasts, fights, and dances that come with a meal.

On the wall, a calendar's stuck in last spring,
Marking the day when the tuna could sing.
Each scratch and scuff a tale to behold,
Of mishaps and laughter that'll never grow old.

The fridge, an odd poet, lists grocery woes,
Inverse recipes from way back in prose.
A roll of an orange and a laugh so bright,
Chasing dreams down the hall, into the night.

In the corners, a landscape of all that remains,
Of fortunes in tiles and their playful refrains.
A mosaic of life where humor prevails,
In this house of delight, where every heart sails.

Forgotten Voices Resurfacing

In the attic, dust resides,
Old laughter still subsides,
A cat in a hat takes a glance,
And dances in a silly prance.

Walls listen to secrets grand,
Of paper planes and rubber bands,
Nerf guns shooting, giggles loud,
Echoes of a playful crowd.

Beneath the creak of every floor,
There's a tale that begs for more,
An old shoe holding wishes dear,
And sock puppets packed with cheer.

Each crack holds a cheeky grin,
Of fights with pillows, bubbles win,
Graffiti scribbled, hearts aflame,
A history of silly games.

Treasures in the Quiet Corners

In the shadows, whispers thrive,
A dusty doll begins to jive,
Marbles tumble, a carnival hue,
A rubber chicken, oh what a view!

The couch, once a space of grace,
Hides crumbs from every race,
Silly notes and candy wraps,
Here lies joy, in secret laps.

Forgotten toys spin tales anew,
Of pirate ships and skies so blue,
Cupcakes made from dirt and leaves,
And tall tales that the mind believes.

In closets stacked, mem'ries bind,
Giggles echo, pure and kind,
Every corner, a goldmine laugh,
A photograph of the past's graph.

Monochromatic Chronicles

Colors fade but stories glow,
Beneath the paint, the echoes flow,
A polka-dotted elephant grins wide,
While a rubber duck takes a slide.

Splashes of cringe in every hue,
Walls painted with "I love you,"
Each stripe tells of clumsy chores,
Like the time we splashed in stores.

The gray of age can't dull the sound,
Of whispered giggles all around,
A sequin dream in monochrome,
Where laughter feels just like home.

Faded prints and crayon scrawls,
Echo the fun of playful brawls,
Past splendor in dreary sight,
Turns mundane into pure delight.

The Layers We Leave Behind

Nostalgic whispers in the air,
Peeking through, a kitten's stare,
Beneath the layers of dust and lore,
Lie memories of "just one more!"

Old journals speak of terrible rhymes,
And secret crushes through the times,
Stickers stuck on every slip,
An ode to every friendship trip.

Forgotten socks and lingering smells,
Piling stories of jokes and jells,
Stuck in corners, wrapped in cheer,
The messiness we hid, oh dear!

In photographs all piled high,
Are snapshots of laughter, oh my!
The layers hold, in every seam,
A chaos that inspires dreams.

The Unseen Chronicles of Rooms

In the attic lies a sneaky mouse,
He hosts wild parties in a tiny house.
Dust bunnies dance to a tune so sweet,
While old pictures gossip, oh what a treat!

The couch has dreams of a grand old play,
Where cushions plotted to run away.
Lamps pretend they're stars with all their might,
Casting shadows that giggle in the night.

The fridge hums jokes, ice cubes in a whirl,
As leftovers strike a comedic twirl.
Cabinets hold secrets, a dish drops low,
With frosted memories of last week's show.

So listen close to the stories told,
In corners where treasures and laughter unfold.
For every nook has a tale to share,
In the heart of a home, there's always flair!

Tales Stitching Across Generations

Grandma's quilt hides patches of cheer,
Each stitch a memory, oh so dear.
Poking fingers as they thread and weave,
Spinning stories, we can hardly believe!

A rocking chair creaks with tales of old,
As granddad spins yarns both clever and bold.
Kids gather 'round, their eyes open wide,
Laughing and gasping at the things they hide.

The old piano plays a familiar tune,
Keys tickle toes like a wild raccoon.
Each note a giggle, a memory flies,
While cats in the corner roll eyes and sighs.

So gather your kin, share a chuckle or two,
For laughter's glue in the quilt that's true.
With each story shared, the fabric grows strong,
Binding us together in this merry song!

The Palette of Human Experience

In the kitchen, colors swirl and blend,
Sauce splatters dance, they just can't pretend.
Spatulas giggle with their culinary flair,
While spices gossip, what's cooking? I swear!

The walls wear paint, a shade of bold fun,
Covered in laughter, a masterpiece done.
TVs blare sitcoms, laughter on repeat,
As playful cats leap, ever so fleet.

In the yard, flowers share their bright lines,
Spreading tales of honey and sunshine.
Each bloom a performer in the show of life,
Painting joy amidst the everyday strife.

So dip your brush in the palette we keep,
Create your own colors, don't lose sleep.
For every splash crafts a vibrant new tale,
In this gallery of giggles, we shall not fail!

The Breath of Ancient Timber

The old door creaks with a voice of mirth,
Whispering tales of its past on this earth.
Each panel worn, with a story to tell,
Like a remote that knows how to cast a spell!

The beams overhead chuckle in the light,
Tickling the rafters, agreeing outright.
Windows that wink with a draft of fun,
Sharing secrets like two mischievous ones.

Even the floorboards giggle and sway,
As little toes stomp to the rhythm of play.
"Don't step here!" they warn with a squeaky cheer,
"Last time we trembled—now that's what I fear!"

So welcome the sighs of the timbered old ghost,
For laughter echoes where memories boast.
In every crack, there's a tale to unfold,
In the warmth of their breath, the young and the old!

Verses Hidden in the Hearth

In the corner, a sock's gone missing,
It danced with the dust bunnies, blissfully hissing.
Underneath the old, creaky chair,
A beetle's waltz, a curious affair.

The fireplace grins with a crackling sound,
As marshmallows launch, oh, so round.
Each charred remains of a burnt-up joke,
Smiles echo louder than any old folk.

A cat prowls, supreme with flair,
While old photos offer a side-eye stare.
"Look at us," whispers the faded frame,
"We wore those outfits, and yes, we're still game!"

Giggles tumble like logs in a pile,
For every chuckle, there's a new style.
The hearth may be quiet, but don't be deceived,
It holds more tales than we've ever believed.

Remnants of Laughter That Linger

Tickling walls with jokes unsaid,
Echoes of laughter, enough to thread.
The wallpaper peels with a cunning grin,
Whispering secrets of where they've been.

The couch has tales of faux pas shared,
With cushions that hug, as if they cared.
Each spill of juice, a giggly tale,
Of messy moments that will prevail.

A lamp that flickers like it's on stage,
Recites old punchlines, in a giggly rage.
"Oh, you thought that was the end?" it beams,
"With a pop and a flick, we'll fulfill your dreams!"

In every nook, remnants of glee,
From pranks and puns, you'd surely agree.
Laughter echoes in the air we breathe,
Remnants stick around, so never leave.

Chronicles of the Weathered Frames

In dusty frames, hilarity lies,
Smirking at life with twinkling eyes.
Old picnics, where sandwiches fought,
For a bite of laughter, they sought and caught.

Each crack in the glass tells a tale,
Of cats on a chase, and foods that went pale.
A distant cousin, grinning wide,
Hunting for snacks, in the picnic tide.

Portraits gathered with hats askew,
Each glaring at humor that's long overdue.
With silly poses, they never got right,
Waving at us, "Come join the delight!"

So gather round these memories bold,
For laughter's the warmth that never grows old.
Through weathered frames and scratches tight,
The chronicles live in our hearts' light.

Portraits of Lives Long Passed

In a gallery of giggles, they hang on the wall,
With bowties that wobble and hats that fall.
Each smile preserved in a canvas frame,
Holds stories of nonsense, yet never the same.

A jester's laugh jumps through the years,
Tickling our fancies, wiping our tears.
Oh, they knew how to dance through the gloom,
While we still find them in every room.

"Remember that time?" the portraits proclaim,
When Grandma's cake turned into a flame?
With a wink of the eye, they invite us in,
Let's relive those moments, let the fun begin!

So toast to the snapshots, the silly parade,
For each flash of joy is a memory made.
Laugh with the frames, and don't let them pass,
For life in each corner is a humorous blast.

Conversations Between the Timbers

In the corner, a chair creaks,
Timbers gossip, sharing weeks.
"Who's that bump?" whispers a beam,
"Just the cat, don't start to scream!"

The door squeaks when it feels bold,
"I've got secrets, wish I could hold!"
A floorboard laughs, 'I've heard it all,'
'That's the sound of old dust's brawl!'

Beams joke softly, 'What a sight,'
'A feather duster's pure delight!'
Chimney chuckles, smoke in the air,
'Is that a ghost? Or just a chair?'

In this house, the stories cling,
Echoes of laughter, hearts that sing.
Timbers chatter, each tale's a gem,
In this wild talk, there's joy for them.

Cracks That Tell of Seasons

Cracks in the wall may seem so sly,
But they've witnessed snowflakes fly.
"Remember when we laughed so loud?"
"Perfectly—just me and the crowd!"

Sunshine creased the summer's heat,
Telling tales of kids with bare feet.
Those little marks, they're not just drafts,
They hold the joy of first belly laughs!

When rain pitter-patters on the roof,
"Dance like ducks!" cries a playful hoof.
Seasons change, but the cracks all stay,
Collecting whispers in their own way.

Old wallpaper, peeling in style,
Once held parties, made hearts smile.
With every crack, a memory's spun,
Like an old joke that's still just fun.

Murmurs of Forgotten Laughter

The attic is dusty, alive with cheer,
Murmurs from shadows, whispering near.
"What's that? A poltergeist?" they tease,
"Just Grandpa's snoring, please, oh please!"

Old toys left to ponder their fate,
'They were once heroes, now second-rate!'
A doll with a grin, eyes full of fun,
"I've seen things, I know everyone!"

Laughter echoes in the cracks of the floor,
"Remember the time? You fell through the door!"
Stories like bubbles float high in the air,
At dusk, they swarm, beyond compare.

The sun sets, but giggles remain,
In the shadows, they dance again.
Each giggle a treasure, a little delight,
In the murmurs, the world feels just right.

The Heartbeat of Old Foundations

The foundation hums, a bass in the room,
"Got some rhythm, let's banish the gloom!"
Walls thump along, a quirky refrain,
"Keep it down, it's a bit insane!"

Bob the beam shakes, dancing with zest,
"I'm older than you, a true arch-nemesis!"
Floors wiggle, groan, joined in the beat,
"Can't resist this, just move your feet!"

Whispers of wood, in a playful trance,
"Let's start a party; come join the dance!"
Nails rattle with joy, hear their song,
Even the dust knows it won't be long.

Together they jive, this enchanted band,
Foundations humming, oh isn't it grand?
Each creak a chuckle, each sigh a tune,
In the heartbeat of laughter, night ends too soon.

Echoes of Days Gone By

In the attic, dust bunnies play,
Chasing memories that never stray.
Grandma's hats piled high and proud,
Whispering secrets, oh so loud.

A sock puppet comes alive at night,
Telling jokes, what a silly sight!
Curved mustaches from long ago,
Dancing shadows, putting on a show.

Nail holes tell tales of bygone friends,
Where laughter lived, and never ends.
Old toys giggle in the dim light,
In their world, all's fun and bright.

Each crack in the wall, a line of snickers,
Remnants of laughter, sly little flickers.
A time-travel portal, oh so clear,
In this crazy home, we've much to cheer.

Tales Underneath the Stairs

Creepy shadows, or so they say,
Live beneath where we seldom play.
Old shoes whisper wacky lore,
Of running races with a dinosaur!

Brooms have conversations at night,
Arguing whose turn is to take flight.
Dusty ghosts with a penchant for pie,
Challenge each other on who's more spry.

The vacuum chuckles, it's quite absurd,
Claiming it's taken one too many birds!
Spiders spin yarns of wiggly woe,
As crickets hum sweet tunes below.

Underneath the stairs, oh such delight,
Each tale and quirk brings pure delight.
A kooky kingdom where whispers dwell,
In every corner, a tale to tell.

The Canvas of Eons Spent

The wall is a canvas, a laughter spree,
With pink smudges from where Joe got free.
A handprint from a sticky-faced kid,
Explains his escape, wild where he hid.

Bubbles from a gum-chewing pout,
Illustrate moments we laugh about.
Pencil scribbles, a heartfelt plea,
"Mom, I'm a superhero, can't you see?"

Scuffs from the dance of a puppy's paws,
And a smirk from the cat with a tiny claw.
Balloon string remnants, a vibrant hue,
Commemorate parties that joyously flew.

Each inch a tale, spun with delight,
As time stamps swirl in the soft twilight.
A mural of giggles and silly lines,
In the corners, pure joy defines.

Confessions of Timeless Spaces

In the hallway, jackets hold a tease,
Whispers of outings in the breeze.
An umbrella speaks of rainy fights,
And secret crushes on chilly nights.

The clock's tick-tock has grown quite bold,
Histories shared in giggles untold.
The wooden floor creaks an old lullaby,
As memories waltz and softly sigh.

Curtains giggle in the summer sun,
With tales of hide-and-seek fun begun.
A forgotten toy beneath the chair,
Dreams of adventure float through the air.

In timeless spaces, laughter's a thread,
Binding each joy in the stories we've said.
Echoes resound with a comedic flair,
In every crevice, a giggle to share.

Shadows of Forgotten Tales

In the corner, a cat starts to purr,
While the old couch still bears its fur.
Echoes of laughter in a creaky chair,
Whispers of secrets floating in the air.

Cupboards full of dishes, mismatched and bright,
Tell of the dinners that went late in the night.
Grandma's spoon dances, a tap to the beat,
While Grandpa just snores, doesn't miss a treat.

A picture of Uncle, in his polka dot shirt,
Smiling and goofy, oh, was he a flirt!
The wallpaper's peeling, with colors so bold,
For every wrinkle, a story retold.

Windows are winking—who would they spy?
The postman, the kids, or birds passing by?
With a giggle and a sigh, they seem to agree,
Life's a funny show, come sit and see!

The Language of Textured Surfaces

Fingers trace patterns, like tales from old,
Once was a pirate, now just a mold.
A pizza slice stuck, on the fridge's door,
Laughter erupts over legends of yore.

Cracks in the plaster tell of a fall,
When Dad tried to dance at the family hall.
The floorboards creak with each funny step,
A polka routine that none want to prep.

Pots and pans clank, like a jazzy refrain,
In a culinary concert, never mundane.
The fridge hums a tune, as it remains still,
Storing our dreams and leftovers until.

Paintings are crooked, with frames all askew,
Yet they hold memories, some silly, some true.
Here laughter echoes, in a rhythm divine,
With walls that remember, and love intertwined.

Memories Embedded in Brick

Each brick whispers names, some quite absurd,
Like Roger the Rooster, who thought he was heard.
In the garden, gnomes giggle in the sun,
With spades in their hands, ready to run.

Chipped paint on the door tells of shoe scuffles,
When the kids played hide and seek, oh what ruffles!
Ghosts of the past dance on dusty old floors,
With tales of the mishaps and ways they encore.

The old swing set creaks, oh, how it sways!
Echoing laughter that brightened the days.
A raccoon once pilfered some treasures so dear,
Leaving paw prints of mischief year after year.

A small garden patch with carrots untamed,
Bears witness to battles of who was most aimed.
In this jolly abode where memories stick,
Life's comical play is quite the rich pick!

Stories Etched in Silence

The old clock ticks, but can't tell the time,
Caught in a tale that's dressed up in rhyme.
Silent walls chuckle at each little blunder,
As the cat plots mischief with a gaze of thunder.

Faded postcards hang like a gallery show,
Of trips and mishaps where laughter would flow.
On the mantel, a trophy for best plunderer,
A dog named Fido, the family's wanderer.

The attic is filled with treasures so quaint,
Like Grandma's old typewriter that can't even paint.
A dust bunny whispers, "Once I was grand!"
As long-lost stories get lost in the sand.

In the night, when the moon casts her glow,
Hilarious tales from shadows start to grow.
So gather around, for the laughter's our guide,
In this house of yarns, where the stories abide.

Vignettes in the Quietude

In a quiet nook, a cat sits tight,
Whiskers twitching, dreaming of flight.
A squirrel grins, plotting a snack,
While the dog thinks, 'Hey, that's my pack!'

Chairs creak low, gossiping dust,
Old shoes chuckle, 'In us, you trust!'
Paint peels back, sharing its tales,
Of wild parties and elated fails.

A clock winks, counts all the hours,
As a plant sings soft, 'I love these flowers.'
Sunbeams beam, they stretch and sway,
Inviting the shy, to join the play.

Laughter weaves through the cracks in the walls,
Echoes of children, with bouncy balls.
Each moment captured in cozy seams,
Turns the mundane into vivid dreams.

The Dialogues of Distant Echoes

Whispers bounce, a game of tag,
'Did you hear that?' a voice does brag.
An old chair beams, 'Oh, such a scene!'
While wood floors giggle, 'We're all routine.'

Lights flicker on with a cheeky grin,
'Let's take bets, on who'll walk in!'
The wind chimes jingle, sharing glee,
'Watch that cat leap, it's all free-fall spree!'

Framed memories chuckle, a warm embrace,
'Remember that time? Oh, what a face!'
The curtains jump, exposing the light,
'Drama unfolds, come see tonight!'

Echoes linger, stories collide,
A lively dance of past and pride.
In every nook, laughter does roam,
These spirited chats create our home.

Stories from the Heartbeat of the City

Traffic lights chatter, counting the cars,
'Who's the fastest? Come, set the bars!'
Pavements hum tales of lost and found,
While pigeons coo, spreading joy around.

A busker strums, a smile ignites,
The old lamp post sways through the nights.
Sidewalks sigh, 'Let's tell our tale,'
Of cakes and laughter, and the odd dog's wail.

Flags flutter freely, whispering lore,
While window plants gossip, 'Is that a score?'
Banners wave tales of festivals grand,
Inviting all, to take a stand.

Rumbling subways echo, doing their rounds,
Where strangers unite, each heartbeat sounds.
In the city's breath, humor flows wide,
Connecting us all, in the daytime ride.

The Poetry of Ruins

In broken bricks, a poet pinches,
'Did you hear that?' as laughter glitches.
Old vines curl up, with tales to tell,
Of picnics past, and a toaster's swell.

Cracked walls chuckle, a playground scene,
'We host the best, of calm and keen!'
A rusty swing, with an ancient jibe,
'Hey, remember fun? Let's revive the tribe!'

Dust motes dance, a swirling spree,
'Let's paint the past, with glee!'
The moon grins down, 'Oh, what a sight!'
A raucous gathering, turning dark to light.

In ruins, humor and heart embrace,
Each sagging beam, a dancing space.
Stories live on, in whispers bright,
As laughter lingers through the night.

Portraits of the Unseen

In the corner laughs a cat on a frame,
Its whiskers twitch at a neighbor's claim.
A dog in a bowtie, dancing with glee,
Is locked in a gaze with a ghostly decree.

There's a painting of Auntie, knitting away,
While mysteriously, her yarn seems to sway.
With every stitch, she tells a tall tale,
About how her tea turned quite sour with the snail.

A child on a swing, stuck mid-air,
Yells for someone to give him a scare.
The portraits, it seems, have minds of their own,
With secrets and stories that never are shown.

A goofy old grandpa with socks that don't match,
Swears he can barter a fish for a catch.
Oh, the tales these portraits amusingly weave,
Like a cat with a monocle, who just can't believe!

Legacy of Tattered Wallpaper

Once vibrant patterns, now faded and torn,
Whisper of parties, celebrations so worn.
Balloons and confetti in colors that clash,
Now stuck like a sneeze that went off in a flash.

A floral explosion with petals askew,
Where secrets have lingered, and pranksters flew.
Under a smudge, a handprint still glows,
From a climb of a kid who just fancied a pose.

Old wallpaper, you keep all the laughs,
From mischievous kittens to playful mishaps.
What stories you'd tell if only you could,
Of the time little Timmy just hid in the wood!

With every peel, a chuckle is found,
From echoes of voices that bounce all around.
You've seen it all, through grief and delight,
Oh, the legacy you hold, wrapped up tight!

The Breath of Timeworn Boards

Squeaky planks echo, oh what a delight,
They croak like old men in the dim evening light.
Each creak has a tale of the people who tread,
Like a dancing musician who lost his head.

Underneath, if you listen, you'll hear giggles and cheer,
As children once played, without any fear.
A stampede of footsteps, a cat in pursuit,
Of a runaway ball, of a wild little loot.

There's a nagging voice saying, 'clean me today!'
But what's the fun in that, let the dust dance and sway!
Timeworn, yet lively, these boards hold the sound,
Of laughter and mischief that still can astound.

We tiptoe around like we're playing a game,
Avoiding a sneeze that heralds our shame.
Oh, the breath of these boards has stories so bright,
Each step ignites memories, a delight!

Hushed Voices in the Atrium

In the atrium's glow, a whispering breeze,
Tickles the curtains, puts hearts at ease.
A forgotten plant, leaning to chat,
With a wind that giggles, saying, 'Isn't he fat?'

The chandelier sparkles like stars that conspire,
To eavesdrop on laughter, and spark a desire.
'Hey, did you hear about the cat in a coat?'
Who tried to outswim a very small boat?

Sounds bounce like rubber, they giggle and bounce,
With each creak and crack, you'll hear every pounce.
The walls lean in close, with glee in the room,
As stories unfurl like a soft, fragrant bloom.

In the corners, they chuckle, these voices of past,
Echoes of joy that forever will last.
Oh, what fun it is to linger right here,
With hushed voices swirling, it feels so sincere!

The Dialogues of History

In the corner, a whispering chair,
Sharing secrets with the worn-out air.
Paint drips like gossip from the past,
Every scratch and dent, a story cast.

The creaky floorboards know the dance,
Of every jest and every glance.
A.N.T.A.R.C.T.I.C vision of paint that peels,
Laughing at memories no one steals.

The old lamp flickers, tells a joke,
Of past mishaps, of laughter's cloak.
Echoes of voices, in playful cheer,
Making history feel like it's near.

So, let's stroll down this hallway wild,
Where time plays games, and walls have smiled.
Each crack, a grin, each shadow, a jest,
Listening closely to history's best.

Voices Embraced by Structure

A brick bows down, quite proudly, you'll see,
It stirs up tales with glee, oh so free.
The window grins, a frame for the show,
As curtains flutter, the wispy winds blow.

The pipes hum a tune, odd but sincere,
With laughter echoing, 'Can you hear?'
They wiggle and giggle in playful beats,
Crafting symphonies with creaks and wheats.

Remember that vase that once took a dive?
Now it holds stories, feeling quite alive.
It chuckles, "Why not just break and rebirth?"
A funny reminder of laughter's worth.

So gather 'round, let's hear every chime,
Of walls that jest in space and time.
For every corner hides a quirky spin,
In structures that hold us, let the fun begin!

Time's Canvas of Moments

A splash of color on a wall so bare,
Brushed with a memory, held with care.
The stairs creak softly, a rhythm of fun,
As dust bunnies laugh, 'Oh, here comes the sun!'

Paint splatters whisper, 'What a wild day!'
While a cat in the corner just lounges away.
The old clock chuckles, 'Tick-tock, what's next?'
In this gallery of time, we feel quite perplexed.

With each tick of time spinning tales like slinkies,
Grins from the shadows, old friends, not stinky.
The floor tiles chuckle, 'Remember that dance?'
A jig through ages, giving life a chance.

So here we are, with laughter as paint,
Scribbling joy on moments we can't faint.
Each hue a wink, each shade a delight,
In the canvas of time, let's laugh through the night.

The Archive of Echoed Laughter

A shelf full of wisdom, an echoing giggle,
As old as the books that forever wiggle.
Beneath a stack of paper, a smirk does reside,
Guarding the tales that once lived with pride.

The desk lamp winks, casting soft shadows,
It nudges the notes where laughter still glows.
A clearly defined timeline with blips of glee,
Wrinkles in pages from stories set free.

The teacup whispers, 'Do you recall?'
Of tea parties gone by, the jokes, and the brawl.
With every sip, a chuckle unspooled,
In this archive of echo, we've all been schooled.

So flip through the laughter, the joy, and the cheer,
In corners, in cracks, all the things that we hear.
A collection of smiles, aged like fine wine,
In the archive of echoes, laughter will shine.

Quiet Testimonies of the Heart

In shadows cast by old wooden chairs,
The secrets of whispers dance in pairs.
A cat naps loudly on the old rug,
Dreams of grand feasts and a warm mug.

Dust bunnies gossip beneath the light,
While chairs are waltzing, oh what a sight!
A squirrel in windows, eyeing the treats,
Skeptical of humans and their strange feats.

A picture hangs crooked, in utter disgrace,
It's been like that since a pie hit the face.
With laughter echoing from sun-laden nooks,
Old tales come alive in scrapbooks and books.

Laughs turn to memories with glee and cheer,
In corners where laughter is louder than fear!
So toast to the tales that these rooms do share,
For every heartbeat leaves whispers of care.

The Recollections of Yellowed Paper

Old letters lie nestled in forgotten drawers,
With ink so faded, they're hard to score.
A love note from '42'—quite a mess,
Did Grandma truly think that's how to impress?

The paper's crinkled, like my sense of style,
Yet it holds moments that make me smile.
A shopping list turned novel, oh what a plot,
With 'milk' and 'eggs'—the drama's red hot!

Stains of coffee map the destiny sought,
Did Dad aim for the mug? He certainly fought!
Recipes written in a gooey embrace,
"Just a pinch of this," an artful disgrace!

So here's to the papers that quirkily talk,
Like an old friend sharing tales while we walk.
May the stories of yesteryear always amuse,
In wrinkled yellow pages, there's no room to snooze!

Scars of Time on Stone Faces

The stones appear grumpy, etched with time's tale,
They're like old men telling tales never pale.
A chip here, a crack there, a face full of quips,
Decades of laughter, and some unforeseen slips.

Graffiti scribbles like a laugh from a friend,
Or some wild child just writing to bend.
A heart and initials in vibrant pink spray,
Love's funny trajectory in a topsy-turvy way.

Pigeons gossip above with serious flair,
As if they know secrets best kept in the air.
Each flake of paint tells a not-so-fine tale,
Of storms and sunrises, making all male.

Oh, these stone faces, rough and robust,
Guard stories that shimmer—yes, in them we trust!
To the past they are linked, but oh how they jest,
With every chip and blemish, they banter the best!

The Memoirs of Weathered Windows

Windows squint from the weight of the years,
Their panes speak whispers, giggles, and cheers.
As the dust bunnies twirl in a dance of delight,
Old curtains join in, a glamorous sight!

They've seen lovers kiss and kids run about,
The same spot where once a cat thought to pout.
These glassy-eyed watchers know all of the fuss,
Like eavesdropping ghosts that silently discuss.

Summer storms painted with lines of strong rain,
Best friends with the broom, they've felt every pain.
But come autumn's chill and winter's freeze,
They keep the laughs warm, like a long cozy tease!

So raise a glass to the windows that gleam,
In their funny little world, life's a grand dream.
Through their colorful tales, we find silly grace,
A panorama of moments, in this whimsical space!

Silent Witnesses of Time

In corners, secrets whisper low,
The tattered wallpaper puts on a show.
A cat once slipped, the dog took flight,
While grandpa claimed it was quite a sight.

The floorboards creak with every joke,
As if they're sharing tales bespoke.
A runaway shoe, a sock so bold,
The story's better when humor's told.

When mice hold court on the kitchen ledge,
They debate each crumb with a regal pledge.
The moldy cheese, it's quite a prize,
To snack on as they plot and rise.

Oh, the light bulb flickers, like it's in on the fun,
While shadows dance like they've just begun.
This house, alive with laughter and cheer,
Holds knit together every quip year by year.

Parables of the Crumbling Corners

In a creaky nook, an old chair sighs,
With stories of naps and some zany highs.
A dust bunny's court holds trials galore,
The verdict? Uneaten crumbs on the floor.

A broken shelf holds a clock that's stuck,
Time laughs at us, oh what bad luck!
While the pots and pans join in a band,
Making music only they can understand.

Sticky notes tell tales of days gone by,
Of burned toast and pancakes that seem to fly.
The fridge hums softly, a sage in disguise,
Holding mysteries between the cheese and pies.

The wallpaper peels like an onion's tears,
As if it's been here for many years.
Yet, there's humor woven in every crack,
For every story has a silly smack!

Ageless Echoes in Stillness

In silence, clocks tick with a punchline or two,
While echoes linger, as if they knew.
The old rug chuckles at every fall,
As stories bounce off the chipped wall.

With windows that peek at the silliest sights,
They've seen nosy neighbors in late-night fights.
A bird that mistakenly flew in for a snack,
Has surely left laughter and a bit of wrack.

Each picture frames a grin gone awry,
With photos of moments that make you cry.
A long-lost sock and a wayward cap,
Once proud in their place, but now in a nap.

Voices of ages hum a light tune,
As if the past knows how to festoon.
Walls wave hello with a joyfully grin,
As laughter seeps through the places we've been.

Reflections on Shattered Glass

In shards upon the floor, a chaotic dance,
Each piece reflects a misfit romance.
A light bulb smashed during a cooking spree,
Has tales more wild than most could foresee.

The windowpane tells of storms gone awry,
With raindrops giggling as they flop by.
While the mirror, cracked, shows a quirky face,
That's aged like fine wine, yet runs in the race.

Beneath the chaos, humor aligns,
With every stumble, surprise defines.
A tattered curtain twirls, feeling grand,
As if it's a dancer, in high demand.

At dusk, when shadows start their parade,
The glass fragments gleam like a prank well-played.
They laugh at the tales of a well-worn strife,
For even in cracks, there's a joyful life.

www.ingramcontent.com/pod-product-compliance
Lightning Source LLC
Chambersburg PA
CBHW062108280426
43661CB00086B/319